www.sphinxtheatre.co.uk

Sphinx Theatre Company presents

Hans Christian Andersen's

the little mermaid

adapted by Pam Gems

First performance: 23 September 2004
Greenwich Theatre, Greenwich, London

Sphinx Theatre Company presents

Hans Christian Andersen's

the little mermaid

adapted by Pam Gems

The thing that is surprising about the stories of Hans Christian Andersen is the same thing that is surprising about all fairy stories – the darkness. There is fright, there is cruelty, there is helplessness – all of which are conditions of childhood. You are smaller than they are. You are in their power (which is why lifting a hand to a child is so patently impermissible). But fairy stories endure. Why? Because they are true, and none more so than the stories of Hans Christian Andersen.

Theatre exists to supply the imagination. It is not for the insolence of pronouncement, of exhortation. Theatre is where we leave off, go somewhere else – relate, not through instruction or precept – but through feeling. Rene Descartes, the French philosopher, said 'Feeling Is Thinking', when you feel you are pierced to the heart. All great work, whether painting, music or literature, has the quality of pang – of instant perception, enlargement of the spirit... of wonder. And no-one has a more unerring aim for the truth of feeling than Hans Christian Andersen. His work is full of darkness... and the light, the consolation of truth and spiritual wholeness.

Pam Gems, July 2004

Cast

Undine	Lydia Fox
King Triton/King Mawlprat	Jami Quarrell
Florestan/Scuttle/The Seahorse	Philip Cumbus
Selusine/Queen Fatua	Sue Bruce
Melusine/Humble/Princess Serenissima	Michaela O'Connor
Queen Pearl/The Sea-Witch/Princess Idia	Cassandra Friend

Production credits

Director	Sue Parrish
Designer	Liz Cooke
Composer	Howard Davidson
Lighting Designer	Chris Davey
Choreographer	Dominic Leclerc
Associate Choreographer	Jami Quarrell
Production Manager	Jim Leaver
Company Stage Manager	Steve Cressy
Deputy Stage Manager	Caroline Weavis
Assistant Stage Manager	Nikki Kitts
Wardrobe Supervisor	Jools Osborne
Marketing and Press (national tour)	Mark Slaughter Associates
Press (London)	Martin Shippen
Production photographs	Robert Day
Publicity design	Emma Cooke
Casting Director	Julia Horan CDG

Special thanks go to: Robyn Simpson, Alexandra Moen and Kim Romer

Biographies

Lydia Fox Undine

Lydia recently played the part of Samantha in *Holy Terror* for the Ambassador Theatre Group. Other theatre includes Viola in *Twelfth Night,* Creation Theatre Company; Juliet in *Romeo and Juliet*, Marlow Society; Alice Bragg in *Tony Ponzi Presents* (Edinburgh Festival). Film includes *Home from Home* and *Perambulans.* Television includes *Garth Marenghi*.

Jami Quarrell King Triton / King Mawlprat

Jami has come full circle from acting through dance, physical theatre and circus returning to acting in the season of Late Plays with the Royal Shakespeare Company at the Roundhouse, London. He could not have been in better hands in returning to his original love of acting, being directed by a trio of British Theatre Giants – Michael Boyd, Matthew Warchus and Adrian Noble. He has recently returned from the southern hemisphere where he taught Indian and Aboriginal children through Cirque du Soleil's global outreach programme (Cirque du Monde). He joins Sphinx as an actor and Associate Choreographer alongside Dominic Leclerc. This has delighted Jami as he rarely gets to wear both hats in one production.

Philip Cumbus Florestan/Scuttle/The Seahorse

Graduating from RADA this year, Philip's most recent appearance has been in a new play, *The Soldier*, based on the life of Rupert Brooke (2004 Edinburgh Fringe). Roles at RADA included Neil in *Speaking in Tongues*; Marius in *Marius*; Raleigh in *Journey's End*; Tyler in *The Schoolmistress*; Stanley in *A Streetcar Named Desire*; and Richard in *Richard III*. Television and radio includes *A Touch of Frost*; *Hope and Glory*; *My Hero*; and *Our Brave Boys* for Radio 4.

Sue Bruce Selusine/Queen Fatua/ Anemone

Sue is a dancer, choreographer, aerial performer and teacher. Armed with a Dance degree from Coventry University and championship competition experience in sports acrobatics, she recently completed a national tour of *The Ice Pack* with Exponential Aerial Theatre. Other circus experience includes *Circ Chicane*, directed by Deborah Pope and Skinning The Cat's U.K tour including the *2002 Commonwealth Games*. After working professionally with Susanne Thomas and Topiary Dance, Sue directed/choreographed work for Warwick Arts Centre and Edinburgh Fringe, combining dance, poetry, physical theatre and a symphony orchestra. Sue is in international demand as an aerialist, stilt walker and fire performer.

Michaela O'Connor Melusine/Humble/Princess Serenissima

Originally from Melbourne Australia, Michaela trained at the Circus Space in London. Her credits include *The Millennium Dome Central Show*; *Storm* (UK/German Tour); *Ganagstars* (UK Tour) both with The Generating Company of which she is a founder member; *The Baron in the Trees* for Scarabeus (Faeroe Islands); *White* (More London Building). Michaela performs in many corporate events and galas including Princes Trust (Highgrove); Royal Courts of Justice; Glastonbury; and Delhi, India. Most recently she performed in *The Gruffalo* with Tall Stories (Broadway/US tour).

Cassandra Friend Queen Pearl/The Sea-Witch/Princess Idia

Cassandra trained at Ecole Jacques Lecoq. Her work in theatre includes *Gentlemen Volunteers*; *Shut Eye*; *The Lucia Joyce Cabaret*; *The Snow Queen* and *The Tragedy of Joan of Arc* for Pig Iron Theatre Company. *Bond* for Theatre O (National Tour); *Tabletop Tragedies* for Ken Campbell (The Barbican); *Mr China's Son* (The Pleasance). *Dido, Queen of Carthage* and *The Round Dance* for Angels in Architecture. TV includes *Jack Dee's Happy Hour*; *Badger* and *Love or Money*. She also tours nationally as the compere for *Sing-a-long-a Sound of Music*.

Pam Gems Writer

Pam Gems many plays include: *Piaf* (SWET Award, RSC, West End and Broadway); *Queen Christina* (RSC); *Loving Women* (Arts Theatre); *Pasionaria* (Newcastle Playhouse); *Aunt Mary* (Donmar Warehouse and New York); *Camille* (RSC, Stratford); *The Danton Affair* (RSC Barbican); *The Blue Angel* (fRSC and West End); *Stanley*, Olivier Award and Evening Standard Award for Best Play (National Theatre, New York); *Marlene* (West End, national and tour of Europe) and *The Snow Palace* (Tricycle Theatre). Pam's many translation credits include *A Doll's House* (Newcastle); *Uncle Vanya* (Hampstead Theatre and National Theatre); *The Seagull* (National Theatre); *Ghosts* (Cardiff) and *Lady From The Sea*, which re-opened the Almeida Theatre in 2003.

Sue Parrish Director

Sue Parrish has been Artistic Director of Sphinx Theatre Company since 1990. Trained as a ballet dancer, she began her theatre career as an Arts Council Trainee Director at the Half Moon Theatre in London, has run her own company and was appointed Associate Director at Greenwich Theatre 1989/90. She is the current Chair of the Theatre Committee at the Directors Guild of Great Britain. Sue has produced all of Sphinx's recent national and international tours, as well as the Company's conferences and seminars. Recent directing credits include: *Hamlet* by William Shakespeare; *Playhouse Creatures* by April de Angelis; *Black Sail, White Sail* by Helene Cixous; *Hanjo* by Seami and Mishima; *Voyage In The Dark* by Jean Rhys; *Sweet Dreams* by Diane Esguerra; *Cherished Disappointments in Love* by Jouko and *Juha Turkka* adapted from the Finnish by Bryony Lavery and *As You Like It* William Shakespeare.

Liz Cooke Designer

Liz's extensive theatre credits include: *Round the Home – Revisited* (West End); *Thyestes* (RSC, The Other Place); *Resurrection, The Recruiting Officer* (Lichfield Garrick); *Fledgling* (Circus Bites tour); *Blue* (Old Vic); *Mother Courage* (Graeae Theatre Company tour); *The Accrington Pals* (West Yorkshire Playhouse); *And All the Children Cried* (West Yorkshire Playhouse/ New End/ BAC Time Out Critic's Choice); *The Birds* (RNT); *Green Field* (Traverse); *The Magic Toyshop* (Shared Experience); *Destination* (Volcano Theatre Company); *The Hackney Office*, *The Spirit of Annie Ross* (Druid Theatre Company); *Spoonface Steinberg* (Sheffield/ New Ambassador/ Kennedy Centre Washington); *Cooking With Elvis* (Live/ Whitehall Theatre);*The Glory of Living* (Royal Court Upstairs). Opera credits include: *Don Giovanni*, *Carmen* and *La Traviata* (Holland Park Festival).

Howard Davidson Composer

Howard Davidson is a prolific composer of music for film, television, radio and the theatre and is in great demand for both drama and documentary scores with over three hundred to his credit, including many orchestral scores performed by the BBC Concert Orchestra, and both the Royal Philharmonic and Philharmonia Orchestras. Recent theatre productions include *Vita and Virginia* by Eileen Atkins, *After Mrs. Rochester* and *Madame Bovary* for Shared Experience. Radio credits include Iris Murdoch's *Under the Net* and Nabakov's *Laughter in the Dark*, and for television Michael Wood's *In search of Shakespeare* and *White King, Red Gold, Black Death* for the BBC2 Storyville strand.

Chris Davey Lighting Designer

Design credits include *One Flew Over the Cuckoo's Nest* (Gielgud Theatre); *Iphiginia at Aulis* (National Theatre); *Yellowman* (Everyman Liverpool/ Hampstead); *Earthly Paradise* (Almeida Theatre); *Rattle of a Simple Man* (Comedy); *Beasts and Beauties* (Bristol Old Vic); *The Quare Fellow* (Oxford Stage Company); *The Sugar Syndrome, Crazyblackmuthaf***inself* , *The Force of Change* (Royal Court), *21* Rambert Dance Company, *The Vagina Monologues* (National Tour), *My One and Only* (Piccadilly and Chichester), *Dangerous Corner* (Garrick), *The Car Man* AMP (Best Musical Event Evening Standard), *Honk!* (National Tour), *Closer* (Abbey Dublin), *Baby Doll* (Albery, RNT, Birmingham Rep), *In a Little World of Our Own, Endgame* (Donmar Warehouse), *Blood Wedding, Grimm Tales* (Young Vic).

Dominic Leclerc Choreographer

Dominic is currently Resident Director of Sheffield Theatres where he is working with Michael Grandage. Recent work includes: *A Christmas Carol* (Assistant Director to Neil Bartlett, Lyric Hammersmith); *The Birds* (Assistant Director to Kathryn Hunter) and *His Dark Materials (*Assistant Director to Nicholas Hytner) both at the National Theatre. Other credits include: *Heavenly* (Frantic Assembly); *Insomnia*; *Witness Me*; *Dystopia* (National Student Drama Festival Awards, including a Director's Award); *Innocence* (BAC); *Blue* (Old Vic); *Agamemnon* (The Point, Southampton); *Fledgling* (Riverside Studios/UK Tour); *Protect Me From What I Want* (Young Vic); *Circelation* (Arts Council project). Performing credits include: *Train in Gallery with Sunflowers* (Topiary Dance Company); *Ghetto* (Library Theatre Manchester) and *Painting with Colour* (Pleasance, London).

For Sphinx Theatre Company

Artistic Director   Sue Parrish
General Manager   Susannah Kraft
Administrator   Bonnie Mitchell
Financial Administrator   Mary Armstrong
Director Sphinx Writers Group Clare Lizzimore

Sphinx was founded nearly thirty years ago and has played a proud and historic role in British theatre since it inception. The company tours nationally and internationally, specialising in producing new work by established and emerging women artists. There is scarcely a woman writer writing in the theatre today who has not worked with the company, or who has not been touched by its pioneering activities. The Company tours new work on the mid-scale, with more experimental, studio based work on the small-scale, often bringing shows into London as part of a national tour.

Sphinx gratefully acknowledges support from the Arts Council, and thanks to Gander & White Shipping Ltd for sponsorship in kind.

Sphinx Theatre Company
25 Short St, London SE1 8LJ
0207 401 9993/4

Sphinx Theatre
Registered Charity No: 279627
admin@sphinxtheatre.demon.co.uk
www.sphinxtheatre.co.uk

Sphinx Past Productions

1973	*Instrument for Love* by Jennifer Phillips
	The Amiable Courtship of Miz Venus and Wild Bill by Pam Gems
	Lovefood by Dinah Brook
	Mal de Mère by Micheline Wandor
	Parade of Cats by Jane Wibberly
1974	*Fantasia* by the company
1975/6	*My Mother Says I Never Should* by the company
1976/7	*Work to Rôle* by the Company
1977	*Out on the Costa del Trico* by the company
1977/8	*Pretty Ugly* by the company
	In Our Way by the company
1978/9	*Hot Spot* by Eileen Fairweather and Melissa Murray
1978	*Soap Opera* by Donna Franceschild
1979/80	*The Wild Bunch* by Bryony Lavery
1979	*My Mkinga* by the company
1980/1	*Better a Live Pompey than a Dead Cyril* by Claire McIntyre & Stephanie Nunn
	Breaking Through by Timberlake Wertenbaker
1981	*New Anatomies* by Timberlake Wertenbaker
1982	*Time Pieces* by Lou Wakefield and the company
	Double Vision by Libby Mason
1983	*Love and Dissent* by Elisabeth Bond
	Dear Girl by Libby Mason and Tierl Thompson
1984	*Trade Secrets* by Jacqui Shapiro
1984/5	*Pax* by Deborah Levy
1985	*Anywhere to Anywhere* by Joyce Halliday
	Witchcraze by Bryony Lavery
1986	*Fixed Deal* by Paulette Randall
	Our Lady by Deborah Levy
1987	*Holding the Reins* by the company
	Lear's Daughters by Elaine Feinstein, with the company
1988	*Picture Palace* by Winsome Pinnock
1989	*Pinchdice & Co.* by Julie Wilkinson
	Zerri's Choice by Sandra Yaw
1990	*Mortal* by Maro Green and Caroline Griffin
	Her Aching Heart by Bryony Lavery
1990	*Christmas Without Herods* by Lisa Evans
1992	*The Roaring Girl's Hamlet* by Shakespeare, in a setting by Claire Luckham
1992/3	*Every Bit Of It* by Jackie Kay
1993	*Playhouse Creatures* by April De Angelis
1994	*Chandralekha* by Amrit Wilson
	Black Sail White Sail by Héléne Cixous
1995	*Hanjo* by Seami, adapted by Diane Esguerra, Yukio Mishima and trans. Donald Keene
1996	*Voyage in the Dark* by Jean Rhys, adapted by Joan Wiles
1997	*Goliath* by Bryony Lavery based on the book by Beatrix Campbell; (Nichola McAuliffe nominated for TMA / Barclays Best Actress Award 1997)

1998	*The Snow Palace* by Pam Gems (Nominated for TMA/ Barclays Best New Play Award 1998)
1999	*Vita & Virginia* by Eileen Atkins, based on the correspondence of Virginia Woolf and Vita Sackville-West
1999 / 2000	*Sweet Dreams* by Diane Esguerra
2000/01	*A Wedding Story* by Bryony Lavery
2001	*Cherished Disappointments in Love*, by Jouko and Juha Turkka adapted from the Finnish by Bryony Lavery
2002	*Sweet Dreams*, adapted from her original play by Diane Esguerra for an Education Tour
2003	*As You Like It* by William Shakespeare
2004	*The Little Mermaid* adapted by Pam Gems from the story by Hans Christian Andersen

Pam Gems

THE LITTLE MERMAID

OBERON BOOKS
LONDON

WWW.OBERONBOOKS.COM

First published in 2004 by Oberon Books Ltd
521 Caledonian Road, London N7 9RH
Tel: +44 (0) 20 7607 3637 / Fax: +44 (0) 20 7607 3629
e-mail: info@oberonbooks.com
www.oberonbooks.com

Reprinted in 2016

A catalogue record for this book is available from the British
Library.

ISBN: 9781840024876
E ISBN: 9781849437912

Cover image by Emma Cook

Printed and bound by Marston Book Services, Didcot.
eBook conversion by CPI Group (UK) Ltd, Croydon, CR0 4YY.

Visit www.oberonbooks.com to read more about all our books
and to buy them. You will also find features, author interviews and
news of any author events, and you can sign up for e-newsletters
so that you're always first to hear about our new releases.

Introduction: Fairy Tales R Us

What is surprising about the stories of Hans Christian Andersen is what is surprising about all fairy stories…the darkness. There is fright, there is cruelty, there is helplessness – all of which are conditions of childhood. You are smaller than they are. You are in their power (which is why lifting a hand to a child is so patently impermissible).

But fairy stories endure. Why? Because they are true. And none more so than the stories of Hans Christian Andersen.

The challenges of doing a stage version of *The Little Mermaid* for a modern audience are to do with period. The original *Little Mermaid* is suffused with the Christian morality of 150 years ago. How to transpose orthodoxies of another era without traducing intention? And how to produce a version for children and adults with enough action for the young and enough insight to hold the attention of their parents? To some extent this solves itself since, though we grow up, the child within does not go away (if it does we are in trouble, depleted, if not worse). What matters can be sought by exploring what theatre is for.

Theatre exists to supply the imagination. It is not for the insolence of pronouncement, of exhortation. Theatre is where we leave off, go somewhere else – relate, not through instruction or precept – but through feeling. René Descartes, the French philosopher, said, 'Feeling is thinking. When you feel you are pierced to the heart.' All great work, whether painting, music or literature has this quality of pang – of instant perception, enlargement of the spirit… of wonder. And no one has a more unerring aim for the truth of feeling than Hans Christian Andersen. His work is full of darkness… and the light, the consolation of truth and spiritual wholeness.

Pam Gems

Characters

UNDINE

KING TRITON

QUEEN PEARL

SELUSINE

MERLINE

PRINCE FLORESTAN

SCUTTLE

STARFISH

OCTOPUS

SEAHORSE

SEA ANEMONE

HUMBLE

KING MAWLPRAT

QUEEN FATUA

PRINCESS IDIA

PRINCESS SERENISSIMA

SEA WITCH

Cast Requirements: 6 Actors (4F, 2M)

ACT ONE

Scene One

THE SEA PALACE.

A strange, beautiful world where everything moves slightly – huge flowers which act as canopies on long stems, shining ribbons of seaweed – sand, and one enormous conch shell with a gaping pink interior.

Music and sound, rhythmic and relaxing. Then a burst of sound as SELUSINE and MERLINE run through laughing. They have shimmering, flexible tails and walk with little steps on feet like tiny iridescent fins. Peace once more and the soft shadows of moving fish. Then UNDINE, the little mermaid, emerges from the conch shell. She pauses and listens to make sure that she is alone, then crosses and sweeps aside a high mass of green ribbon seaweed, pinning it back swiftly and expertly and covertly, as if she has done it before. She reveals a beautiful marble statue of a boy in the Greek style. She clears the sand from his feet reverently and sinks down beside him in adoration. She caresses his leg with her cheek and remains, in habitual stillness, so that she, too, is like a statue.

The King, KING TRITON, her father, enters, a majestic but kindly figure in a swirling cloak. He contemplates UNDINE silently and then makes a sea sound, beckoning off. UNDINE looks up as her mother, the beautiful QUEEN PEARL, enters.

QUEEN PEARL: *(Shakes her head.)* Displeasure, Undine.

  UNDINE comes over to the KING.

UNDINE: *(Sweet, singing tone.)* Papa – Mama –

QUEEN PEARL: *(Gently.)* Displeasure.

UNDINE: Papa...

QUEEN PEARL: *(She turns to the KING and then points to the statue.)* Remove?

7

*The KING thinks. He looks from the statue to the QUEEN
to UNDINE, and gestures to the QUEEN 'Is it necessary?'*

Jetsam. Sea litter. Remove.

*The KING plays tenderly with UNDINE'S long, swirling
hair.*

KING TRITON: Undine's toy.

QUEEN PEARL: *(Mildly.)* Indulgent father.

KING TRITON: *(Raises UNDINE, cuddles her.)* Baby girl.

QUEEN PEARL: Baby not, dear Triton. Tomorrow –
birthday!

KING TRITON: Ah – tomorrow! Fifteen!

He smiles down at UNDINE.

QUEEN PEARL: Tomorrow – Undine maiden!

*UNDINE clasps her FATHER needfully then slips from his
grasp, kisses her MOTHER and runs off. They laugh and go.*

Music.

*SCUTTLE, the Sea Chamberlain, enters with high structures
of shells, arranged decoratively for the birthday. He places them
carefully, returns with fat iridescent jelly-fish cushions. He
tries some star-fish scatter cushions – removes the purple ones
as naff – leaves the pale yellow and coral ones. His* pièce de
résistance *is an enormous fan of red coral which he places
behind the throne.*

Music. Music down.

Scene Two

*The KING and QUEEN, splendidly dressed, enter and sit on their
thrones. They watch their daughters SELUSINE and MERLINE
enact a shipwreck. The dumb play ends and the KING and QUEEN*

applaud, but UNDINE, at their feet, rises in sympathy. SELUSINE and MERLINE placate her. The QUEEN smiles fondly, makes a sound. SCUTTLE enters with UNDINE's birthday presents. He presents a Shawl of Light to the QUEEN, a large Gladstone bag made of iridescent fish scales to the KING, and a green, fronded, seaweed collar to SELUSINE and MERLINE. The KING presents UNDINE with the bag and kisses her on both cheeks.

KING TRITON: To dear daughter… Treasure. Guard well.

The QUEEN steps down, envelops UNDINE in the Shawl of Light.

QUEEN PEARL: Undine – safe. Undine – unharmed. My daughter!

UNDINE throws her arms around her MOTHER and they embrace in the clouds of light.

UNDINE: Mother. Thank you.

SELUSINE and MERLINE can't wait to give UNDINE their present. She turns and the shawl seeps away at her feet. SELUSINE puts the beautiful seaweed around UNDINE's neck, arranging the fronds over her breast. MERLINE watches, smiling. Then darts forward and blows gently, and globules of light glow within the seaweed.

SELUSINE: Collar of Love –

MERLINE: Love!

UNDINE claps her hands in delight.

UNDINE: Ah…
Ahh!! Love!

Music. UNDINE kisses the QUEEN and the KING and then stands before him formally. The KING puts a chaplet of jewels, similar to those of her sisters' on her head.

KING TRITON: *(Kisses her.)* Daughter.

The OTHERS embrace her.

Selusine – maiden… *(He kisses her.)* Merline – maiden…
(Kisses her, tickles her, making her laugh.) Undine –
Maiden!

*The sounds of celebration rise, almost to cacophony, making
UNDINE a little fearful.*

SELUSINE: Tomorrow – !

MERLINE: Dawn tomorrow – Aloft!

KING TRITON: Land!

QUEEN PEARL: Sky!

SELUSINE: Air!

MERLINE: Fire!

UNDINE: *(Puzzled.)* Fire? *(Turns to the KING for
explanation.)*

MERLINE: Fire scorch –

UNDINE: *(Puzzled.)* Scorch? *(She turns to her mother.)*

QUEEN PEARL: Fire – pain.

UNDINE: *(To her sisters.)* Pain?

*Her sisters shake their heads. They don't know what it is and
turn to their father.*

KING TRITON: No. Pain no. Tomorrow, daughter Aloft!
Land – humans – people.

Observe, Undine.

Absorb – discover.

And return safely.

*He sprinkles UNDINE with gold dust for safety. The girls
run off happily, bearing the presents.*

QUEEN PEARL: Triton, I fear.

KING TRITON: Beloved no – no fear. Undine fine child.

QUEEN PEARL: Fine *child. Green* maiden.

KING TRITON: *(Smiles.)* Green as all maidens.

QUEEN PEARL: *(Shakes her head.)* Undine different. Deep.

KING TRITON: *(Nods.)* True.

QUEEN PEARL: Wants more.

KING TRITON: Like her mother.

QUEEN PEARL: Oh Triton… *(Takes his hand.)*

KING TRITON: For Triton it was Pearl – Pearl, come what may. *(He takes her hand.)*

Be calm. Undine resourceful. Bright.

QUEEN PEARL: But dreamy.

KING TRITON: Like Pearl – seeking happiness…

QUEEN PEARL: Neptune protect her.

KING TRITON embraces her protectively.

Scene Three

THE SISTERS' BEDCHAMBER.

The girls are in nightdresses made of pale, translucent seaweed. They sit together on a large scallop shell bed.

SELUSINE: *(To UNDINE, protesting.)* Again? Hear again?!

UNDINE: Please!

MERLINE: *(Nudging SELUSINE.)* Say again. For birthday.

SELUSINE: Such much! *(She sighs, makes herself comfortable, plays with her long hair.)*

At first, strange…

UNDINE: Strange? More, please!

SELUSINE: Remembering!

First – moonlight, but not shimmer through wave, through swell. Alive, globe shining, turning sand to gold. And stars!

UNDINE: Stars?

SELUSINE: Jewels of light across emptiness.

UNDINE: To catch?

SELUSINE: No, no, no.

MERLINE: Too far for net.

UNDINE: What more?

MERLINE: Town – houses – streets –

SELUSINE: People!

MERLINE: Such much noise!

MERLINE gives UNDINE some decorative earmuffs made of giant cockle shells – putting them on to display them.

SELUSINE: Creatures! *(She barks like a dog.)*

MERLINE moos like a cow and then baas like a sheep.

MERLINE: And Things! *(She and SELUSINE sigh in happy memory.)*

SELUSINE: Shops…

MERLINE: Hats…

MERLINE: Shoes…

UNDINE: Shoes?

MERLINE: For feet.

SELUSINE: Big ugly platters below.

SELUSINE: Snowboots – winklepickers – *(Baffling UNDINE.)*

MERLINE: Flip flops –

UNDINE: Flip flops?

SELUSINE: *(Dreamy.)* Such much.

UNDINE: Best? Best of all?

MERLINE: Oh – Chocolate! *(Points to her mouth, leans forward, growls.)* Chocolate…

UNDINE: *(Draws back.)* Chocolate frightening?

MERLINE: Oh yes!

SELUSINE: No!

Merline!

They have a brief pillow fight.

Pax.

MERLINE: Pax.

They settle down.

SELUSINE: Bed now.

MERLINE: *(Whispers to UNDINE as the girls lie side by side.)* Soon over, aloft. Soon tire. More fun home.

SELUSINE: Don't spoil.

MERLINE: Humans, ugh!

SELUSINE: *(Nudges UNDINE, indicating MERLINE.)* Went too close.

MERLINE: *(To SELUSINE.)* Spit on you.

SELUSINE: See?

MERLINE: Two-legged beings awkward.

SELUSINE: *(Puzzled.)* No fins.

MERLINE: No scales.

UNDINE, in the middle, looks from one to the other.

SELUSINE: Humans… *(She looks for the word.)*

MERLINE: Ugly.

The GIRLS snuggle down.

UNDINE: *(To herself, puzzled.)* Ugly?
   No.
   Human beings…
   …different.
   Strange.
   Beautiful.

They become sleepy.

UNDINE: *(Murmurs.)* Tomorrow…

SELUSINE: Tomorrow…

MERLINE: *(Murmurs, sleepy.)* Stay deep, Undine.

UNDINE: *(Murmurs.)* Tomorrow…tomorrow…

Music. Lights down.

Scene Four

UNDINE'S RISE TO THE SURFACE.

UNDINE stands alone, composing herself. She crosses her hands on her breasts for an incantation to Neptune. She is wearing the seaweed collar, touches it gravely.

UNDINE: Divine Neptune
   Soften waves –
   Breeze –

Calm Zephyr.

Instruct swell,

Tide,

Ebb, Flow.

Oh Neptune –

Deadliest

Friendliest

Most Important…

Make Maiden

strong…unfearing…

She stands straight and still.

Now!

UNDINE swims aloft to a high receding sound and then blinding light.

Scene Five

THE DECK OF A SHIP.

One gigantic sail. The sound of sweet singing. Sunshine, and a slight, gentle movement of the sails. Fine weather.

The song ends. UNDINE hauls herself on deck. She slides helplessly, then braces herself against a stanchion. She looks around, taking in the ship, eyes wide. And is startled by the sound of a hatch being opened.

PRINCE FLORESTAN comes on deck. He is like UNDINE's Greek statue. UNDINE falls in love.

The PRINCE goes to the rail, looks out to sea, and skywards, inspecting the weather.

PRINCE: *(Calls.)* The wind's shifted! *(Louder.)* Storm on the horizon – take in sail!

The stage darkens. A storm. Loud thunder, lightning – shouts, mens voices crying for help, calling for their mothers. Sounds of the ship breaking up. By the light from the lightning flashes we see the PRINCE felled by a spar, and UNDINE hauling the PRINCE to safety.

The sounds fade to silence.

Scene Six

THE SHORE.

UNDINE, on her stomach, hauls the PRINCE ashore. She removes his scarf from his neck, wipes his face with her hair, chafes his hands. He is cold. She doesn't know what to do. She pulls the seaweed collar from her neck, places it on his chest. She bends, blows gently. The seaweed comes to life and the golden globules within it glow. The PRINCE stirs. UNDINE bends and kisses his lips. He opens his eyes and gazes into her face. Panicked, she slithers away behind a rock.

The PRINCE sits up, dazed, and leans against the rock. UNDINE watches anxiously. A pause.

Then she cranes forward as the PRINCE, regaining his strength, rises to his feet and stretches his arms wide to the sun. Absently he pulls the seaweed from his neck, allows it to drop from his hand.

PRINCE: Dear Lord, I am delivered.

Oh my poor ship! My shipmates!

Cruel, cruel sea. Pray God they survived.

He goes.

UNDINE: Beloved Neptune –

Safe – safe!

SELUSINE and MERLINE: *(Off.)* Undine –

Undine –

Undine!

UNDINE waves out to them, joyous and unafraid.

Scene Seven

KING TRITON'S PALACE.

The Feast of Shellfish.

SELUSINE enters as a lobster and does a lobster dance. Harmonious applause.

MERLINE comes on as an oyster and dances cheerfully, snapping her shells. Applause.

MERLINE: *(Calls.)* Undine!

SELUSINE: Undine!

> *To fill the gap the KING does his crab dance, despite the QUEEN'S sigh. He teases her into the dance, plonks a mussel bivalve shell on her head and they do a stately cat-walk.*

KING TRITON: *(Breathless.)* Cockleshell!
(Calls.) Cockleshell?

SELUSINE: *(Calls.)* Undine – Cockleshell?

MERLINE: *(Together.)* Cockleshell?

> *But UNDINE does not appear. The QUEEN looks at the KING, rises and crosses to the seaweed-wreathed statue, reveals UNDINE at his feet.*

> *Light change. Later.*

> *A STARFISH enters with a hostess trolley. All eat except UNDINE.*

QUEEN PEARL: *(To UNDINE.)* Eat, Undine. Seawrack soup – good.

> *But UNDINE shakes her head.*

QUEEN PEARL: *(Concerned.)* Ahh…Collysquit?

> *UNDINE shakes her head. She pats her chest. The KING, alarmed, beckons her, puts his ear to her chest.*

KING TRITON: Ship's bell – fine heart!

UNDINE: Feel – feel – *(But she cannot describe her feelings.)*

QUEEN PEARL: Pain?

UNDINE: *(Nods, understanding the meaning of the word.)*
Pain.

The QUEEN turns to the KING.

QUEEN PEARL: *(Points.)* Beautiful boy – out! Undine –
(She points aloft.) – tell.

Pause.

KING TRITON: Undine? Tell. What saw? Tell.

UNDINE: Saw sand – starfish – rock pool.

QUEEN PEARL: And?

UNDINE: Sky.

QUEEN PEARL: And?

UNDINE: Cloud.

QUEEN PEARL: And?

UNDINE: *(Dreamy.)* Sun.
On face.
Warm. *(She puts out a hand.)*

QUEEN PEARL: Saw – who?
Saw who, Undine?
Who warm?

UNDINE pats the statue.

QUEEN PEARL: Saw boy?
Undine?

UNDINE: Warm.

She jumps up and topples the statue over. And stands, weeping. The QUEEN enfolds her.

QUEEN PEARL: Poor Undine.

Poor daughter.

UNDINE: I want.

QUEEN PEARL: Want only what can be, child.

KING TRITON: Undine. Listen.

Here, live 300 years. Up aloft, only 50.

UNDINE: Fifty? Oh! Poor Prince!

QUEEN PEARL: Ah! Prince!

KING TRITON: *(To QUEEN.)* Shipwreck. One saved.

QUEEN PEARL: One saved?

Undine?

Boy saved?

UNDINE nods shyly.

QUEEN PEARL: Ah.

UNDINE: Fifty years! Poor Prince!

QUEEN PEARL: But consolation. Prince human, has soul
– immortal soul.

UNDINE: *(Puzzled.)* Papa?

KING TRITON: Here – 300 years and never more.
Cut like rush – finish. No soul. For Prince – soul lives –
rises to other worlds.

UNDINE: Can see soul?

QUEEN PEARL: No. Invisible.

Forget Prince. Forget aloft.

Be wise.

SELUSINE: Forget –

MERLINE: Forget!

UNDINE: Body warm.

So warm.

QUEEN PEARL: You speak?

UNDINE: *(Shakes her head.)* Kiss mouth.

Eyes open! – he rises!

Legs – so fine.

Human –

Alive!

QUEEN PEARL: On earth alive.

In depth

Where Undine lives

Prince drowns.

Undine – forget.

Misalliance.

KING TRITON: The King forbids.

Forget.

The QUEEN rises, claps her hands.

QUEEN PEARL: Children. Birthday!

SELUSINE: *(To UNDINE.)* Birthday!

MERLINE: Tonight ball!

KING TRITON: Welcome, Maiden!

Feast!

Dance!

UNDINE runs off. The OTHERS leave separately.

Sounds of music being tuned in preparation for birthday ball.

The KING crosses in his combinations attended by an OCTOPUS with choice of clothing. SELUSINE and MERLINE run across the stage in their small-clothes, pursued by a camp SEAHORSE hairdresser. The QUEEN enters and is draped in majestic red and green ribbons encrusted with jewelled barnacles by a nervous SEA ANEMONE.

Scene Eight

The SEAHORSE is doing MERLINE's hair. UNDINE sits on the bed in her petticoat, dangling her legs, her head down. MERLINE gives her a worried look.

MERLINE: *(To UNDINE.)* Forget!

Tonight, fine Mermen –

SEAHORSE: *(In admiration.)* Ahh!

Best cavers – explorers –

SEA ANEMONE: Divers –

SEAHORSE: Synchronized sand-skiers!

MERLINE: Dance, Undine! –

SEA ANEMONE: Sing –

SEAHORSE: Flirt!

MERLINE: Forget aloft. Be happy.

UNDINE: How?

MERLINE: Birthday!

SEAHORSE: Birthday!

MERLINE: Papa has wine from wreck – golden bubbles of light.

SEAHORSE: Warm!

SEA ANEMONE: Warm…

SEAHORSE: Ooh!

SEA ANEMONE: Ooh! *(Reels slightly.)*

UNDINE: Warm?

Here?

Warm?

She jumps off the bed.

The bells ring, and then a clarion call to announce the start of the ball. MERLINE hurries to be ready.

MERLINE: Undine?

UNDINE waves her to go, nods, as if agreeing to follow. She goes followed by the SEAHORSE whom she waves away as he waves a large comb and hairspray at her. Only the SEA ANEMONE is left, waving gently. Sounds of music and cheering and laughter.

The sounds die away to silence.

UNDINE: Anemone…

The ANEMONE shimmers forward shyly, UNDINE'S ballgown in her arms. She proffers the dress. UNDINE shakes her head. Anxious, turning her head nervously to the exit, ANEMONE offers the dress again with a pleading smile, lays down the gown reverently, smoothing out the creases. She stands, hands clasped waiting for instructions obediently. UNDINE looks up at her.

Tell about Sea Witch.

The SEA ANEMONE'S eyes and mouth open wide and she shrinks back in terror.

The Sea Witch.

ANEMONE shakes her head violently – throws herself at UNDINE'S feet.

Strange sounds, low and ominous. UNDINE leans over ANEMONE.

King's daughter. Obey. Tell.

Scene Nine

UNDINE'S JOURNEY TO THE SEA WITCH.

The journey is frightening. Dark shapes loom, there are terrible sounds – roaring and cracking – shrieks of drowning seamen – 'Mother, save me!' – shadows of skeletons – shiny, bleached bones in sudden shafts of eerie light. Sounds lower, pitch darkness.

Suddenly, a dreadful, enormous, open-mouthed fish fills the stage. And engulfs UNDINE.

Scene Ten

THE HOUSE OF THE SEA WITCH.

The house of the SEA WITCH is open-fronted and constructed of the BONES AND SKULLS OF DEAD SAILORS.

Strange sounds – the creaking of foundering boats – dull booms far off – little squeaking sounds, like rats.

Pause.

UNDINE enters fearfully. She carries her Gladstone bag birthday present. It is heavy. She puts it down. And looks about her.

Nervously she approaches a CAULDRON which smoulders and erupts.
She blenches and draws back.
And becomes still –thinking that she hears something.
She looks around but there is no-one.
Just as she relaxes slightly, the SEA WITCH appears from nowhere.

UNDINE screams.

The SEA WITCH is mesmerisingly frightening.

She fixes UNDINE with a Gorgon stare – approaches slowly and prowls around her on a voyage of inspection.
UNDINE flinches as the SEA WITCH peers, close. And steps back.

SEA WITCH: I've seen this face before.

> *She hisses at UNDINE.*
> *UNDINE shakes her head vigorously*

Name?

> *UNDINE tries to speak. The SEA WITCH observes her and understands.*

Oh.

> *The SEA WITCH turns aside, picks up a small flask – thrusts it at UNDINE.*

Talk-spit. Drink! *(UNDINE is puzzled.)* Human-speak – no Mer language here.

> *She gestures forcefully, so UNDINE knocks back the contents of the flask.*
> *And gasps.*
> *And then she bursts into incredibly rapid speech.*

UNDINE: Good morning how do you do please forgive me uninvited guests such a bore shall I wait outside? whatever you prefer I do apologise I've been travelling for so long I don't know which day or night or…

SEA WITCH: Slow down!

UNDINE: *(Not stopping.)* …where or up or down I've lost track my name is Undine, I'm here on a quest for help and assistance in a matter of some importance to me, and if I could explain…

SEA WITCH: Shut up! You were supposed to sip – not slosh it back like a Pompey whore!

> *She gives UNDINE water. UNDINE sips.*

THE LITTLE MERMAID: ACT ONE

What do you want?

She crosses to the cauldron. And disappears. UNDINE looks around, alarmed.

(From behind UNDINE, making her jump.) Well?

Pause.

UNDINE: I want to be human.

The SEA WITCH lets out a terrifying screech.

SEA WITCH: Human? She wants to be human! *(Laughs.)*

UNDINE nods fervently.

What for?

She approaches, indicating with hands which have live creatures for fingers.

(Indicating the bones of the dead sailors.) Look around – here they are. Much good being human did them!

She slurps from a bottle of dark green liquid which emits fumes. And leans forward, smiling evilly.

I know all about humans.

UNDINE flinches.

(Confidential whisper.) How do you think I know? Heh? Heh?

UNDINE draws back.

The SEA WITCH reaches out, grabs a sailor's wooden leg with shoe still attached, smites a large thigh in the wall of her house at her side.

Dad!

The old man. Father, Papa, head of the house, *(Screeching with laughter.)* first mate – very successful mariner my Father.

Up until.

She sits back, belching.

Laugh?

Best ever spawning in the China seas. Pater leans over
– sea like glass – there's Mater shining up vhrough the
swell, sliding over on the crest of a wave – casual…all
it took was a toss of the head, he was over the side like
a bucket of night-soil. Consummation instantaneous,
then one half-hitch of her black hair round his neck and
straight down he goes to Davy Jones locker, eyes on
stalks, tongue waving like a moray eel – mind you, he
was a fine figure of a man – see the buttocks on him –
we had them for Sunday brunch.

UNDINE: *(Faint.)* May I go now?

SEA WITCH: Shut up.

We've heard of you. That rat Triton's daughter aren't
you?

UNDINE: Yes.

SEA WITCH: Lost your heart, have you?

One look aloft and she behaves like a filleted sea trout.

What's in it for me?

*UNDINE turns and bends. And drags forward the beautiful
Gladstone bag. She tips out a large heap of treasure – gold and
silver objects and mountains of jewellery. The SEA WITCH
leaps down and forages, inspecting chalices, throwing necklaces
around her neck – trying a heavy turquoise belt – testing gold
with her teeth.*

Well, well.

You're a little tea leaf, aren't you? Chip off the old block.

UNDINE: I don't know what you mean, it's my inheritance.

SEA WITCH: *(Mocking her.)* 'It's my inheritance.'

Mmm.

We-ell.

Nothing special.

Done!

She shakes UNDINE'S hand, causing an audible crack.

Sorry.

She grabs a live octopus, squeezes it on UNDINE'S hand, mending it.

UNDINE: Thank you. Will you help me?

SEA WITCH: Sure. Okey dokey. Fair trade's no robbery.

She hawks and spits noisily, draws her seat closer and contemplates UNDINE like a beautician deciding on a makeover.

(In a good humour, with many glances at the treasure.) 'Well, all right!'

You want to be human. I can do that for you and why not, since it'll make you more miserable than you've ever known, that being the human condition.

Not my favourite people, your family. I'll do it with pleasure.

She blows her nose on her fingers, wipes her hand on her chest informally.

Human eh?

That means legs.

You want legs, eh?

UNDINE: Yes!

Please.

SEA WITCH: Stumps instead of a beautiful tail. So that the prince will fall in love, marry you and give you an immortal soul into the bargain, that being the rule.

She laughs so much she falls off her seat.

'Well all right!'

Sit down. *(As UNDINE rises, nervous.)*

The SEA WITCH, muttering to herself throughout, prepares a potion.

Stand back.

The cauldron gives a firework display. Each time they think it is over the cauldron fizzes and pops again, but at last it is silent. The SEA WITCH dips in a finger and tastes.

Mm.

The SEA WITCH fetches a jug, decants some of the decoction into a bottle, corking it firmly. She hands it to UNDINE, who grasps it eagerly.

Now listen. At dawn, swim aloft. Be on the shore as the sun touches the horizon and drink this.

UNDINE: All of it?

SEA WITCH: All of it, and don't throw up. Hold your nose, get it down, lie back and brace yourself. When the pain starts, think of what you're doing it for, and if that doesn't work, think of your father and your mother, who'll love you whatever you look like – and DON'T LOOK DOWN.

UNDINE: Pain?

SEA WITCH: *(Succulently.)* Oh yes! Humans? In love – and no pain? Remember. Sit still, grit your teeth, it'll be like swords going through you but don't let out a sound. The pain'll come in waves, stronger and stronger, and you won't be able to stand it, but what are you going to do? Dive back into healing salt water? You've got no tail.

When it gets beyond bearing close your eyes with the

sun on your face, with a bit of luck you'll faint and when you come to it'll be all over…that's if I've got it right and you don't end up with stumps or a peg leg.

Have you got all that?

UNDINE: *(Faintly.)* Yes…

SEA WITCH: If I'm up to snuff you'll have the loveliest pair of legs in the whole kingdom – he won't be able to take his eyes off them.

UNDINE: Will I be able to dance?

SEA WITCH: Dance? You'll be the best dancer they've ever seen.

UNDINE: I'll be able to dance with him?

SEA WITCH: Yes! Of course you'll be dancing on knives, in your own blood.

UNDINE: *(Frightened, but rallies.)* But I'll dance with the Prince?

SEA WITCH: That's the deal.

UNDINE: And I'll have an immortal soul like him? So that we can be together forever.

SEA WITCH: If he loves you, and marries you. Turns down all the rich princesses they keep importing for him to look at. If he doesn't marry you – ppft! Finish! You disappear into a lick of foam on the edge of a wave…no body, no life and no soul. You do know what you're doing? Loving's one thing – being loved is another. Plenty of rivals for a Prince and what's so special about you, even with great legs.

UNDINE: I'll take my chance.

SEA WITCH: Gamble, eh? *(Sucks her teeth.)* The odds aren't amazing.

UNDINE: That's true.

Nonetheless, I must go forward.

SEA WITCH: Sure, are you?

UNDINE: I can do no other.

SEA WITCH: *(Sourly.)* For love.

UNDINE: For love. When I came on the deck of his ship
…when I saw the Prince, something was decided.
By me? I can't say. By whom? Certainly not the Prince,
I was hidden, he never saw me. But then the storm, as
if pre-ordained, and I saved his life and it was not easy
and I lost strength and almost dived with his dear form
to have at least his beautiful bones for company. But I
found the strength, Mistress Sea Witch, and hauled him
up the strand, half-drowned, unconscious in my arms,
my limbs so weak and trembling that I could not have
pulled him another inch. It must all be for something.

SEA WITCH: Well – you'll find out.

UNDINE: Thank you. From the bottom of my heart.
(She makes a slight curtsy, turns to go.)

SEA WITCH: Hang on. I haven't finished. I need your
tongue.

UNDINE: My tongue?

SEA WITCH: Give it here.

UNDINE: No!

SEA WITCH: Give me your tongue or the deal's off.

UNDINE: But without a tongue how will I sing to the
Prince?

Woo him with sweet sound?

Converse – amuse – inspire him.

What would I have to offer?

THE LITTLE MERMAID: ACT ONE

SEA WITCH: Your legs, your eyes, your smile, your hair, your breasts, what more does a man want? A woman who talks? Never. Come here.

She bites off UNDINE'S tongue and eats it.

Now buzz off.

Screeching sounds and the SEA WITCH disappears in a huge puff of purple smoke.

UNDINE is alone – bloody-mouthed, clutching the bottle of liquid. She makes piteous sounds. Bravely she moves off to make her journey.

Darkness. Low roaring sounds. UNDINE fights her way through a forest of thick black waving stems. She moves on doggedly.

UNDINE wading in mud which threatens to engulf her.

UNDINE in the dark, moaning soft, breathless moans of fear and exhaustion.

Slow light from above. Silence. UNDINE appears. She kneels to pray to Neptune. But can make only grunting sounds. In anguish she lifts her arms, opens her mouth wide. And then blows.

The word Neptune appears, created out of bubbles and hovers above her. UNDINE composes herself, grasps the bottle in her arms tightly, and is born aloft into blinding light, the Neptune of bubbles rising above her.

ACT TWO

Scene One

THE SHORE.

The sun appears, first as a red sliver on the horizon, and then rising, becoming a radiant yellow disc. And UNDINE is borne ashore on a gentle, rippling wave. She pulls herself up the sand and lies back, exhausted by the journey, against a rock. She closes her eyes to the sun and then opens them. She bends forward and looks down at her tail, caressing it fondly with both hands. She gazes yearningly out to sea, listening to the soft murmur of the waves. She sits very still like the little mermaid on the rock in Copenhagen – a statue. Then she drops her head for a long moment. Turning – she sees the scarf that she had removed from the Prince's neck and laid on the rock. She reaches for it, holds it close, smells it, then kisses it.

She rips the bottle from her neck, throws back her head and drinks. And gags. She gasps, groans, gags again, takes deep shuddering breaths. And keeps the liquid down. Then her body is convulsed as the stage darkens to the rumble of thunder. She arches back, rears and contorts, moans – and faints.

Silence.

Sunlight once more.

Birdsong. A church bell, distant.

UNDINE revives slowly. She lifts her head, groaning softly. She sits up. And lets out a weird, prolonged howl. Her fish tail is an abandoned heap.

She leans forward.

And touches her legs.

Holding on to the rocks for support, UNDINE hauls herself to her feet.

UNDINE: Ah! *(Of wonder.)*

> *She takes a step.*

UNDINE: Ah! *(Of agony.)*

> *She takes stiff paces, groaning with each step.*

> *Soft music.*

> *UNDINE begins to dance, her long hair her only garment. She moves slowly and gently to the music.*

> *Above her, the PRINCE shades his eyes, cranes to see.*

> *The PRINCE approaches from a distance.*

> *UNDINE dances.*

> *The PRINCE approaches. And catches UNDINE as she wheels and falls in a faint.*

> *The PRINCE lifts UNDINE in his arms and walks away with her. The music modulates to the lulling murmur of the waves.*

Scene Two

THE PALACE.

The PRINCE enters, crosses swiftly bearing UNDINE in his arms.

A peremptory and raucous trumpet call. HUMBLE, a slave, runs on backwards, sweeping dust away at the crouch. QUEEN FATUA, extraordinarily dressed, enters.

QUEEN FATUA: *(Calls, irritably.)* His Majestay! His Majestay!

> *KING MAWLPRAT enters hastily, hitching up his braces. HUMBLE runs off, returns with the King's jacket, ruff, shoes and crown – he hangs the crown on the back of the throne.*

KING MAWLPRAT: Sorry Petal – trying for a dump.

QUEEN FATUA: Language, Mawlprat! Still constipated?

KING MAWLPRAT: *(Nods his head.)* We live in
hope. Steady the Buffs, never say die… I'll try the
acupuncture.

QUEEN FATUA: *(Shakes her head, calls to HUMBLE.)*
Stewed rhubarb!…

HUMBLE nods, runs off.

KING MAWLPRAT: Have a heart.

QUEEN FATUA: …or colonic irrigation. What's it to be?

KING MAWLPRAT: Neither, I mean both. Whatever you
say, Petal. Must keep that sunny smile on your face.

QUEEN FATUA: A Queen never smiles.

KING MAWLPRAT: Oh – why ever not?

QUEEN FATUA: Wrinkles!

KING MAWLPRAT: Oh. Oh dear. *(He tries to compose his
face to smoothness.)* How do you stop them?

QUEEN FATUA: Keep out of it.

KING MAWLPRAT: Out of what?

QUEEN FATUA: Everything.

KING MAWLPRAT: Come on. You enjoyed the play last
night.

QUEEN FATUA: It was all right, if you like laughing.
(Shrieks.) Humble!

HUMBLE hurtles on.

HUMBLE: What, Missus?

She clouts him to the floor.

HUMBLE: Ooh, I forgot – the List! *(Runs off.)*

QUEEN FATUA: The List!

KING MAWLPRAT: I'll put some mustard on your bunions, pet. They're looking agitated.

QUEEN FATUA: What do you expect? They think you haven't got ears to hear. Yesterday – *that word* – *five times*!

KING MAWLPRAT: What word, lover?

QUEEN FATUA: The U word!

KING MAWLPRAT: U word? U word? Ooh, let me see, I love games – Uncle – no, we killed him – ugly –

She gives him a clip round the ear.

KING MAWLPRAT: Understanding – no – ubermensch – utterly butterly, up, up and away, Umpty Dumpty, ush little baby don't you cry –

QUEEN FATUA: Usurper!

KING MAWLPRAT: Oh. See what you mean, Petal. Want me to do a few more in?

QUEEN FATUA: *(Snarls.)* No, it's Charm Week – *(Grabs the List from HUMBLE as he rushes in.)* I want you on that balcony chucking out coins day and night.

KING MAWLPRAT: Gold? Silver?

QUEEN FATUA: Kopeks you prat. The coffers are empty. We are broke – skint – cleaned out – what do you think this is for? *(Waving the List at him.)* We must have an alliance – a merger! These are the front-runners – we've taken out all the dogs. *(She unrolls the scroll and reads.)* Cynthia of Serbia. Oh, fat ass. *(She reads.)* There's that little Princess with the ginger hair. Nah – Belgian. Lady Clementine Spruce. Too tall. Princess Pippita of Pop. Too short. The Dowager Queen of Split – she'll be lucky.

KING MAWLPRAT: The Lady *is* loaded, Petal.

QUEEN FATUA: She's past it! We need heirs to kick off a dynasty, get some authenticity going, we can't mess about busking for much longer, we need a Wedding!

KING MAWLPRAT: Jolly good.

QUEEN FATUA: Here's one. Princess Idia from – *(She peers.)* – where's that?

KING MAWLPRAT: *(Looks.)* No idea. Bloody good portfolio, though – oh, I know, they're the snobs from across the Blue Mountains – good wheeze, she's an only child – we'll cop for the lot, bingo.

QUEEN FATUA: Okeydoke, she'll do. *(Shrieks.)* Humble! Set this one up for next Tuesday – full naus – parades, fireworks, the lot. Oh – and tell the Prince.

Scene Three

Another part of the Palace – THE PRINCE'S QUARTERS.

UNDINE, simply but beautifully dressed, sits on a low parapet gazing out to sea. She turns and smiles happily as the PRINCE appears and watches him fondly as he divests himself of his fencing gear.

PRINCE: Beloved child, are you well?

She nods, smiling and runs to fetch his jacket for him.

Thank you. *(Putting on his jacket.)* May I get you something? They've been looking after you?

She nods with a small murmur of assent.

Oh, if only you could speak! There is so much – so much I want to ask you. Were you able to write down your story for me – who you are – where you came from? Were you shipwrecked?

Are you alone in the world? Have you always been dumb?

UNDINE picks up a book and hands it to him.

Oh! Thank you! Now – through the magic of pen and paper we can converse. May I?

UNDINE smiles assent. The PRINCE sits, knees up, on the bench below the balustrade and starts to read. UNDINE moves away, watches him fondly as he twists a lock of hair as he reads.

'My name is Undine.

I came from' – what? – the depths? What does that mean? Oh, you mean from the forests over the mountains…

(He reads on.) 'I chose to leave my home and my loving family to be near you.'

To be near me? But we've never met – not until I found you on the beach – cold and still and picked you up in my arms –

It is odd.

I do seem to know you.

It *is* as though we've met.

He gazes across at her.

I know – it's your eyes!

He jumps down and approaches UNDINE.

Like glowing lapis with streaks of malachite – blue as sapphires and green as grass. Have we met before?
Where?
Where did we meet?

But UNDINE turns away. The PRINCE returns to the book and reads aloud once more.

'I ask only to serve you for the rest of my days. I ask only to love – with hope, or without hope.'

Oh my dear girl.

He crosses, pulls her down and sits beside her.

I shall care for you always. Be assured. Your home is here, in the Palace – as the Prince's ward – and as the Prince's friend. *(UNDINE turns to him, her face alight.)*

(He takes her hand.) You shall never want for a brother's love, dear child.

UNDINE stiffens.

Will that make you happy?

UNDINE'S head is bowed. She nods.

Splendid! *(He rises.)* I must leave you now. *(UNDINE looks up.)*

They want me to marry. *(UNDINE'S face is stricken.)* I know – tiresome, but it needn't affect our friendship – it's a formal thing, an alliance – a marriage of convenience they call it. A merger.

UNDINE shakes her head in shock.

Pooling of assets and – of course – to breed some children, heirs and spares for the kingdom – odd sort of arrangement but there you are. Since the parents over-ran – I mean, took on this place, I have to face certain responsibilities…oh, it will help me so much to have you to talk to, Undine. You are such a wonderful listener!

(As he goes.) And the most wonderful dancer in the world! I shall be honoured if you will dance with me at the Ball tomorrow. *(As she looks up in enquiry.)* To celebrate the arrival of Princess Idia. She's the first on the list. Oh well.

He goes. UNDINE gives way to grief.

Scene Four

THE BALL.

The KING and QUEEN spectacularly overdressed, watch the PRINCE dance with PRINCESS IDIA. Who giggles all the time and is a very bad dancer – the musicians have to keep changing the beat to try and fit in. At the end of the dance the PRINCE escorts the PRINCESS to a seat of honour by the QUEEN, who offers her a box of chocs and watches her scoff, wrenching the box back crossly.

The PRINCE crosses, and bows before UNDINE. They dance, enraging the QUEEN who nudges the PRINCESS who drops the box of chocolates, and barges into the dancing couple, and, as the PRINCE wheels UNDINE away, decks UNDINE, who falls to the floor.

PRINCESS IDIA: Is this your tart?

That's it. We're off!

Who do you think you are? Jumped-up, Johnnie-come-lately bunch of usurpers my father calls you. *(Struggling into a fur coat.)* We should never have accepted this gig. Mother said you were a three-piece suite, satin eiderdown set-up, well you can sod off, the lot of you, I'm off and I'm taking the courtesy gifts with me – and the camels!

She goes, pursued by the aghast KING and QUEEN. The PRINCE and UNDINE dance. She breaks away and he lies on the ground, propped up on his elbows to watch her.

UNDINE dances against the magic deep blue background of the night. As the music volume is lowered we hear the voices of KING TRITON and QUEEN PEARL.

KING TRITON: Dearest child –

QUEEN PEARL: Beloved Undine!

Can it be love?

SELUSINE: Sister – he loves!

MERLINE: He loves Undine!

Music under.

KING TRITON: Praise and honour to Neptune.

QUEEN PEARL: Our daughter will live –

MERLINE: Gain a soul –

SELUSINE: Live for ever!

QUEEN PEARL: Happy, happy Undine...

MERLINE: Live!

SELUSINE: And love – love...

KING TRITON: Beloved daughter...

They call her name, their voices becoming distant.

UNDINE dances. At the end of the dance she and the PRINCE move towards each other, hands outstretched. The PRINCE, entranced, makes to speak.

QUEEN FATUA: *(Offstage.)* The Prince! Where's the Prince?

HUMBLE runs on backwards sweeping the way for the QUEEN.

(Yells, offstage.) Florestan! *(Enters.)* Oh, there you are – *(Hurls him round by the shoulder, pushing him offstage.)* Affairs of state! Affairs of state!

The PRINCE goes, with a last anguished look towards UNDINE.

UNDINE, alone, stands in a pool of blood. From afar, her father and mother and sisters call her name.

Scene Five

UNDINE is sitting in her favourite spot, gazing out to sea. She turns as the PRINCE enters. He crosses to greet her. He is happy and excited.

PRINCE: Oh Undine – oh my dear friend, my dear little friend –

She takes his hand, eager to hear what he has to say.

I have something to tell you. It will please you, I know, for it is joyous news. You will be as delighted to know of my happiness as I should be of yours.

Oh, my dear.

How strange is fortune! Can we know the future? Are patterns laid out for us?

When I found you, with bleeding feet, your hair wrapped around you like soft weed, your face like marble, smooth, as from under the sea, and you opened your eyes – it was as though we knew each other – as though we had met before.

He walks about, full of energy with his news.

I gazed and I gazed and I gazed into your eyes, as I am doing now – as I do every day in this space which you have made so sane and calm and your own –

And the thought of marriage has been repugnant to me. Irrelevant. A distraction from something real.

Until now.

Oh Undine.

The Princess Serenissima of Arcadia has arrived. I come from her now.

Suddenly, suddenly, dear Undine – my memory has been restored!

I remember!

I remember being on board ship – I remember the
storm, the sky darkening – the ship keeling over, the
dreadful noises of timbers cracking – cries of shipmates,
the rush of water, pressure on my ears – darkness –

And then –

The sound of a woman's voice – singing – and being
held aloft and my strength failing and someone,
someone's arms, holding me up, above the waves,
urging me to live.

Then nothing.

And then the sun on my face.

And opening my eyes –

UNDINE comes close, excited.

– and seeing a face of such beauty, eyes so deep, so blue
– blue and green like yours, dearest child – eyes full of
truth – of love, beloved Undine who oh – who has no
need of a tongue to convey virtue, wholeness and grace.

UNDINE puts out her hand in bliss.

Beloved one, I have met her. The girl who saved my
life. As the Princess Serenissima walked across the floor,
and I towards her, to greet each other before the Court
– she looked up, shyly – and I recognised my saviour.
Those same eyes. The colour of the sky. The colour of
the sea. The eyes of truth. I must share my happiness
with you – you of all people –

UNDINE moans softly.

– share the pleasure that it gives me to present you to
my chosen bride, the Princess Serenissima of Arcady.

*He goes to the exit. UNDINE cannot move. The PRINCE
returns with the PRINCESS.*

Beloved. This is my little sister – the orphan I have told
you of, whom I found on the shore.

42

UNDINE dips a small curtsy, swaying slightly. The PRINCESS leans forward kindly, with a steadying hand.

May I present Undine.

PRINCESS: We are happy to know you, Undine, and to see that you are well. If the Prince shall love you, then we shall love you, and we thank you for giving him your loyalty. As we do.

She smiles at the PRINCE, then bends, kisses UNDINE on the cheek.

Tomorrow we sail for home to prepare for our wedding and – dearest Florestan – may Undine be of my retinue? Shall you like that?

PRINCE: Beloved, thank you for the thought. *(To UNDINE.)* You see? How can I not love her? She who saved my life!

PRINCESS: Oh, Florestan – a dream, a magical dream!

PRINCE: You were there. Your soul was there, Serenissima, your soul saved me. I was failing, my strength was spent. Somehow, from somewhere, you held out a hand to me. You lifted me up – you were my rock – my stave in adversity. We were meant to meet. It was ordained.

They hold hands. UNDINE contemplates them and turns, looks out to sea.

And you'll come, little sister? Across the straits to see me married? Share my happiness? You agree? Yes?

UNDINE turns, looks up at him, and nods.

The PRINCE and PRINCESS go. UNDINE collapses, moaning. The sounds are taken up by music. UNDINE raises herself, leans over the parapet. Out at sea, her sisters wave at her, joining in the sounds of lament.

43

SELUSINE and MERLINE: Undine!

Undine!

Undine!

Scene Six

THE SEA WITCH'S LAIR.

The SEA WITCH grinding ingredients in a large pestle and mortar, making horrible grating noises. She suddenly stiffens and turns. KING TRITON is standing there.

SEA WITCH: What are you doing here? What do you want?

KING TRITON: *(Quietly.)* Hullo, Betty.

SEA WITCH: How did you get past the Evil Eye?

What's going on?

She scuttles about, alarmed.

KING TRITON: Wish speak.

SEA WITCH: What? Oh – here –

She throws him a small bottle, similar to the bottle from which UNDINE drank earlier.

Talk human for Hades' sake.

The KING drinks, shakes his head to clear his head of the effect of the potion.

Well?

KING TRITON: Betty, I haven't much time.

SEA WITCH: Get on with it then.

KING TRITON: The young Prince is aboard ship on his way across the straits to be married.

Don't do it, Betty. Don't kill my Undine.

SEA WITCH: Why not?

KING TRITON: Please.

SEA WITCH: She made a bargain.

KING TRITON: You mean, *you* made a bargain.
Did you have to take her tongue?

SEA WITCH: Tongues are trouble. I should know.

KING TRITON: That's all over. Why look back?

SEA WITCH: What do you want me to do? Look forward?
To what?

KING TRITON: Acid corrodes. Look at you, Betty.

SEA WITCH: And if I bathe in the milk of human
kindness I'll suddenly be the family beauty. *(Spits in his face.)* Like my sister?
Ask me?
Me?
The betrayed – the rejected one?
For a favour?

KING TRITON: Please, Betty. If not for me, do it for
yourself. From the goodness of your heart.

SEA WITCH: I have no heart.
You chewed my heart to fragments when you looked at
my sister. You saw her yellow hair and you couldn't take
your eyes off her.

KING TRITON: Who decides feeling?
The heart makes its own demands.

SEA WITCH: How should I know?
I have no heart.

KING TRITON: Please.

The WITCH glares at him, paces, undecided. She walks away, considers, head bent, her back to him. Then, with decision, crosses, forages. And returns. And brandishes a fearsome knife in KING TRITON'S face.

SEA WITCH: Tell her to kill him and bring me his heart. Bring me his heart and she gets a soul and her tongue back.

KING TRITON: You want Undine to kill the Prince?

SEA WITCH: When he puts that ring on another finger your daughter – your baby – becomes foam – lifted in an instant by the wind and blown into nothing… bubbles of air.

His life or hers. Her choice.

KING TRITON: What you suggest is impossible.

SEA WITCH: Are you sure?

Why don't we ask her?

They disappear in green smoke.

Scene Seven

ABOARD SHIP.

Sounds of a sea shanty, followed by cheering and laughter. UNDINE, sheltered by the mast, listens. The sounds die away. Only the creaking of the ship is heard and the soft sound of the wind in the rigging. She closes her eyes and lifts her face to the sun. Opening her eyes she sees the PRINCE and PRINCESS SERENISSIMA on the upper deck. The PRINCE touches SERENISSIMA'S face gently and they walk off. UNDINE can hardly bear it. She walks about, restless and distressed. And makes a sound of fright as she is suddenly confronted by the SEA WITCH.

SEA WITCH: Gave you a little fright, eh? *(She cackles with laughter.)* Thought you might like some company. *(As*

46

UNDINE backs away.) What's the matter? Cat got your
tongue?

(She strides about, convulsed with her own wit.) Got a little
surprise for you. *(Now UNDINE is really frightened.)*

What do you think it is? Go on – guess! Swamp fever?
Foot rot, big, ropy veins all over those beautiful legs?

Would I do that! *(Thoughtfully.)* No.

I've brought something to cheer you up. There she is, I
thought, down in the mouth, all washed up and about to
be snuffed any minute – the girl needs a shot in the arm.

After all, noblesse oblige –

(She bawls, very loud.) Triton!!!

*KING TRITON appears. UNDINE is transfixed with
amazement. And then runs to her father who enfolds her.*

KING TRITON: Dearest, dearest daughter.

UNDINE moans gently.

SEA WITCH: Very touching.

We've got a proposition for you.

UNDINE looks hopefully at her father.

SEA WITCH: He'll tell you.

KING TRITON: What is the point? I already know my
daughter's answer.

SEA WITCH: Before you've put the question?

Ask her!

KING TRITON: And if I do ask her, how is Undine to
answer? You've taken her tongue.

SEA WITCH: Oh, rollicks.

*She puts her hand in her mouth, yanks, and throws a tongue to
UNDINE who gulps and swallows, her hand over her mouth.*

UNDINE: Ahh –

>Ahh – ah
>
>Fa –
>
>Fa –
>
>Father…
>
>Father! *(She embraces her father.)*
>
>Ohh!

SEA WITCH: *(To KING TRITON.)* Get on with it.

KING TRITON: Dearly beloved child. I am constrained to ask you a question. Not of my decision or wish as you will gather. And I know already your response before you speak.

SEA WITCH: *(Snarls.)* Ask the question!

KING TRITON: What is the point?

SEA WITCH: Sure, are you?

KING TRITON: Yes. I am sure. Oh Undine. Better for you to be dumb than for me to hear you accept the dire penalty of a loving heart.

SEA WITCH: Ask the question…ask the question!

>*Silence.*

UNDINE: Father?

>*(Small voice.)* Father?

KING TRITON: Betty – that is, Mistress Sea Witch, has reminded me that if the Prince – if the Prince does not love you, does not want you as his wife, not only will you lose the soul that was promised to you upon marriage to a human, but that you will be dissolved at once into air – light – no longer have being.

>*He falters, trying not to break down. UNDINE puts her arms around him.*

UNDINE: I know, Father.

KING TRITON: But – the –

The Sea Witch offers you your life. And your soul.

UNDINE: My life? My soul?

(Trembling.) How?

The SEA WITCH takes the fearsome knife from behind her back and brandishes it before UNDINE.

SEA WITCH: Kill him.

Kill the Prince, bring me his heart and you can keep your tongue, your soul and your feet won't bleed into your shoes any more.

She advances, and waves the knife hieratically over UNDINE'S head. UNDINE begins to dance, turning slowly, and then more quickly.

UNDINE: *(In wonder.)* No pain!

SEA WITCH: You see?

UNDINE: *(Breathless.)* No pain.

SEA WITCH: Think about it. One swift blow, a couple of twists to open him up, shove your little hand in, grab his heart and away you go – some new clothes and a blonde rinse – what do you say?

UNDINE crosses to her father, kisses him on the cheek.

UNDINE: Beloved father…

She stands before him, shakes her head sadly.

KING TRITON: I know.

SEA WITCH: Look at her, young, beautiful…

You're her father, make her!

KING TRITON: What you ask is impossible, Betty.
As you well know.

This is your revenge. We loved each other, you and I.
But I loved Pearl more.

SEA WITCH: Well – as we see – love destroys.

KING TRITON: Does it?

Does it, Betty?

What about a new deal? A new bargain?

SEA WITCH: It had better be good.

KING TRITON: Terms so attractive you won't be able to
resist.

*He crosses and confronts her. And takes the knife from her
hand.*

I'll kill the Prince.

I'll bring you his heart, put it in this hand *(He takes her
hand.)* in exchange for Undine.

*The SEA WITCH looks up at him, and they remain, staring
intently into each other's eyes.*

SEA WITCH: *(Softly.)* Do it then. *(She whirls swiftly and
points towards the PRINCE who is crossing at a distance.)*

Do it!!

UNDINE: No.

She confronts the SEA WITCH.

UNDINE: *(Quietly.)* If you loved – truly loved my father,
more than yourself, more than life itself, then you would
want and only want his happiness. You would not seek
to destroy him. Whatever the circumstance your only,
eternal and overwhelming need would be to see him
loved, never mind by whom, and living in peace and
harmony. You do not love my father, Mistress. You have
never loved him. If you loved him, truly loved him, you
would not wish him harm. You would wish to protect

him, even if the cost was your own life, or lasting misery every day for ever more.

A life – a soul? Without love?

Where there is love there is no deal.

The SEA WITCH jumps at UNDINE fearsomely, hissing in her face, wheels and grabs the KING by the shoulder as the PRINCE approaches.

SEA WITCH: Kill him!

The KING, stiff-legged and rigid as if in a dream, moves towards the PRINCE who is gazing out to sea. SELUSINE and MERLINE appear from the sea, hand UNDINE her shawl of light.

UNDINE: No! *(She hurls herself in front of the SEA WITCH, brandishing the shawl.)*

Are we to become as you?

Ugly?

(An instruction.) No.

The SEA WITCH makes to attack UNDINE, who throws the shawl over her. The SEA WITCH staggers slightly, reels, confused, begins to moan, clutching her chest. She puts a hand out to UNDINE – who stands firm. With a howl, the SEA WITCH lurches over to the KING as he nears the PRINCE and tears the knife from his hand.

The PRINCE, unawares, moves away.

The SEA WITCH shudders and trembles, muttering and moaning. UNDINE takes the knife from her gently and throws it in the sea. The SEA WITCH collapses, backs away on the deck, sobbing, swathed in the shawl. UNDINE kneels and enfolds her, murmuring comfort. The SEA WITCH rears suddenly in an arching fit. And is still. UNDINE bends over her and then rises and steps back in amazement.

The SEA WITCH rises. She is no longer a frightening sight but a comely woman with long, shining red hair in a green flowing dress.

KING TRITON: Betty?

BETTY: Sorry.

Sorry.

Forgive…

She steps back as UNDINE and the KING move to embrace her. But she is not there. Only the heap of old clothes is left.

Silence but for the soft sounds of the waves.

KING TRITON: The spell is broken.

Ahh!

He staggers slightly, in shock. UNDINE runs to him.

UNDINE: Father!

KING TRITON: *(Clasps her.)* Safe…oh…safe!

They cling together. She looks up at him.

UNDINE: Oh Father – and you were ready to – *(She shudders.)*

KING TRITON shakes his head, dazed.

KING TRITON: Unthinkable. *(He looks down at her.)* Oh Undine, where our children are concerned we are fortune's slaves.

But now, dearest girl – oh, to have you home in the sweet silent realms of the sea where you belong! I will beseech Father Neptune, you shall be restored – a shining mermaid princess as before.

UNDINE: Father –

KING TRITON: Transformation, Undine! It can be arranged, you have my word.

UNDINE: Transformation? *(She moves apart.)*

(Pause.) I was a mermaid.

Now –

Who am I?

What am I?

A human.

With a soul.

A soul, in the name of love.

I lost my love.

But…my love is happy.

So I am happy.

KING TRITON: To become as you were.

UNDINE: Go backwards, Father?

Go back?

No spell on land or sea can command that.

I am nowhere.

Nowhere.

KING TRITON: You are free, Undine. To choose. If not the depths then here. You will not be lost to us.

UNDINE: And I have a soul.

A soul.

To take me – where? That which I sought has been achieved. My beloved will marry – there will be – *(Her voice breaks.)* – there will be children.

But I shall be free. For other worlds. Aloft in the ether, or on the edge of a wave, murmuring in reeds, on mountaintops, or sailing the soft moonlight –

KING TRITON: Merciful Neptune, have pity on us!

Undine!

Must we lose you to thin air – to the whispering tide?

To become a fleeting moment of light, a star's gleam, a
warm breath on a spring morning?

Undine not here?

Not alive?

No!!

UNDINE runs to him.

UNDINE: Beloved Father…

Undine lives –

Undine is here!

And will be. *(She clings to him.)*

Trust…trust.

Life is change.

Oh dearest one, be in me as I am in you. Love me as I
love you and my mother and my sisters and as I love
the depths, and as I love the air and the sky and all who
inhabit the earth and the mighty sea…

Father – wish me well. See me in everything. I shall be
here, watching – seeing – caring for you.

*She turns, and looks up towards the PRINCE and
PRINCESS, who wave at her happily. She waves and they
smile and go, arms about each other.*

*UNDINE curtsies before her father and he puts a hand on
her head and raises her up. She smiles up at him, then turns,
and with a wave of her hand, steps into the air.*

*The KING looks up to follow UNDINE as she climbs the
air. Sea sounds as her name is called, over and over, softly,
from different sources.*

*The ship disappears in a mist of sea and pearly light and soft
pale sky. The sound of singing and music and sea noises and
a ship's bell, from the deep. The sounds swell and fill the air
and then, slowly, they die away to the rhythmic murmur of*

*the waves and we are left with sparkling light on a calm sea,
and the horizon and the blue sky beyond.*

The End.